THE
A–Z
OF
HOMEMADE
LIQUERS

Commissioning Editor Rose Hewlett
Words by Sophie Berry
Illustrations and Design by Zoë Horn Haywood

A

ALCOHOL

Creating delicious and original liqueurs at home is simpler than it sounds. A wonderful array of drinks can be created in your home, with just a few key ingredients and a handful of simple utensils.

The first thing you'll need to source, is of course, alcohol. A good, strong base spirit will be needed, and to this you can add your flavours. Fruits, herbs, spices and sweets work brilliantly when steeped in alcohol, and will give your base spirit a wonderful flavour.

Vodka is a good choice as a base spirit as it is colourless. Gin is also popular, although rum and whisky are good choices, too. You don't need to use the most expensive spirit available, although a base spirit with a high alcohol percentage is preferable.

BOTTLES

One of the most important things on your list
of equipment to source are bottles, and it is
important that you sterilise the bottles that you
use before use. Glass demijohns, Kilner jars, or
large recycled glass bottles are great for making
liqueur in at home, and also look rather lovely.
If you decide to use large bottles or demijohns,
you can always decant your finished liqueur into
smaller, sterilised bottles which will be easier to
serve from.

Sterilisation is a straightforward process, and can
be done easily in the home. First, wash the glass
bottles you are using in very hot soapy water.
Rinse the bottles thoroughly with more hot water,
and then place the glass bottles into an oven on
the lowest heat setting. After 20 minutes, your
bottles will be sterilised, and safe to use. Use the
sterilised bottles while they are still warm.

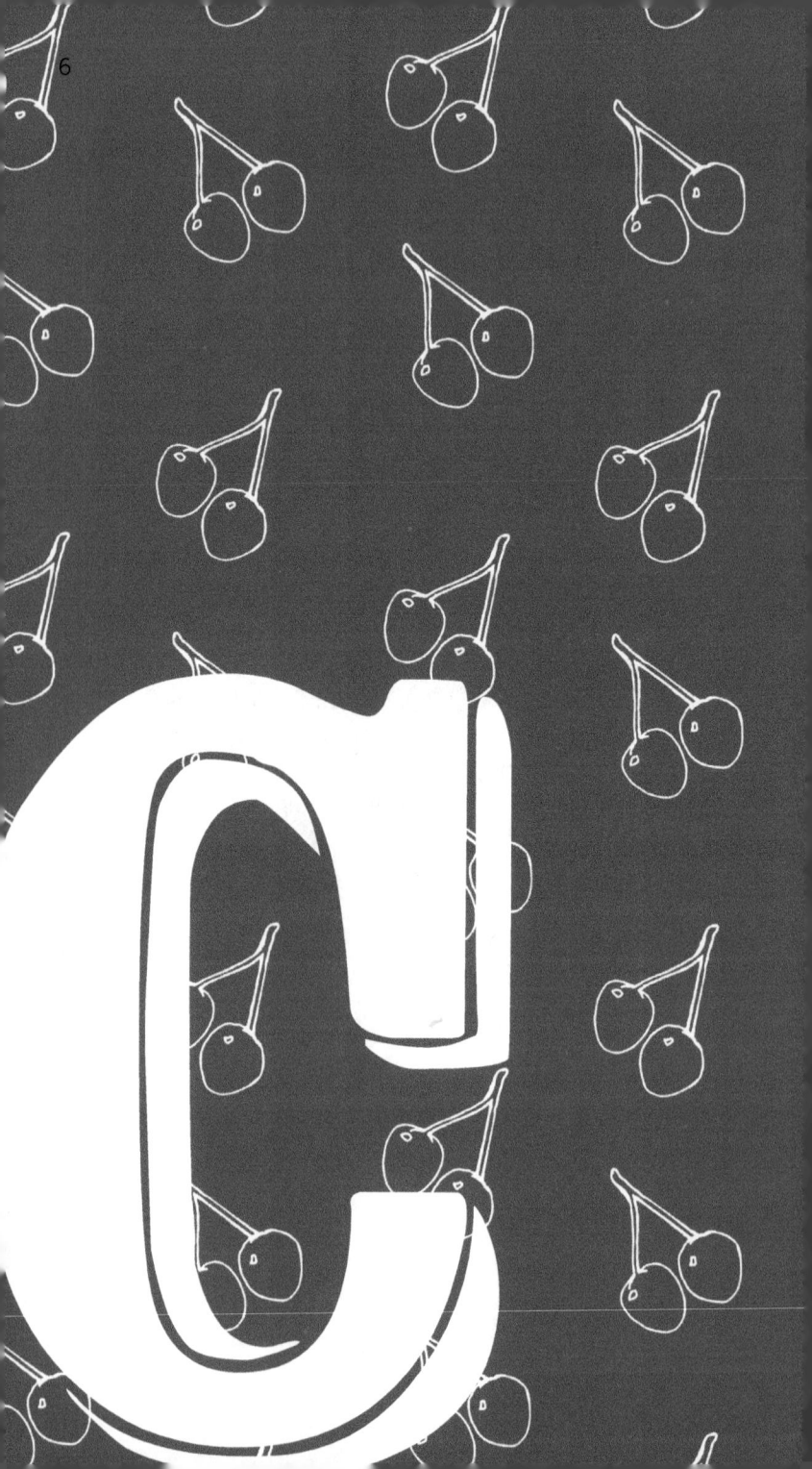

CHERRY

Cherry Bounce is a delicious liqueur which was originally made in a small village called Frithsden, in England. A lane leading from the Old High Street in the nearby town of Hemel Hempstead is even named Cherry Bounce, in tribute to the sweet liqueur. Using a base spirit of brandy, you can make your own cherry liqueur using this classic recipe:

Cherry Brandy

Ingredients
Four cups brandy
1 cup cherries
1 cup sugar

Method
1. Stone and pit the cherries, but do not discard the stones.

2. Place the cherries, stones and sugar into a sterilised bottle.

3. Fill the bottle with brandy and quickly seal the bottle.

4. Leave the cherry brandy to infuse for six months; the longer it is left to infuse, the better the taste will be.

DAMSON GIN

Gin is a wonderful base spirit to start with, as it is clear and holds colour well. It's subtle flavour works well with lots of fruits and herbs added, and damson gin is a great recipe to try. The fruits will give the liqueur a gorgeous deep jewel-like colour, and deliciously syrupy consistency.

Damson Gin

Ingredients
1 lb ripe damsons
4 oz sugar
1 vanilla pod
1 tsp lemon peel
1 cinnamon stick
1 tsp fresh ginger
2 pints gin

Method
1. Carefully place all the ingredients into a large sterilised bottle or demijohn, and top up with gin.

2. Seal your bottle immediately.

3. Allow your liqueur to infuse for at least six months; the longer you leave your liqueur to infuse, the stronger the flavour will be.

4. Filter the liquid through a clean muslin cloth or coffee filter paper before decanting into smaller sterilised bottles to serve.

ETIQUETTE

The rules and rituals of drinking alcohol are numerous, and vary from country to country. From a jolly "cheers!" in England, to an enthusiastic "Sante!" in France, everyone has their favourite ritual when enjoying drinks with friends. From 'wetting the baby's head', to merrily toasting a marriage, a glass of something is the go-to method of celebrating all manner of occasions. Just don't forget to look your friends in the eye as you raise a glass; many a superstitious drinker will insist on eye contact when clinking glasses.

FILTRATION

Filtration is a key part of the liqueur making process. You will find that a number of the recipes in this book will require filtering before the liqueur is ready to serve, so it is recommended that you familiarise yourself with this rather straightforward process.

Filtering out the ingredients you have steeped your alcohol with will leave the flavour and colour of the ingredients behind in the liquid, without any sediment remaining. In some cases, leaving the ingredients too long in the base spirit will result in a bitter taste, as is the case when using tea to make liqueur.

We recommend using a clean muslin cloth, or coffee filter paper and a funnel to filter your liqueur. Simply pour the unfiltered liqueur through your cloth or filter paper and into a clean, sterilised bottle for storing. If you are filtering a liqueur with many small ingredients, such as spices, you may want to repeat the process until you are happy with the clarity of your liqueur.

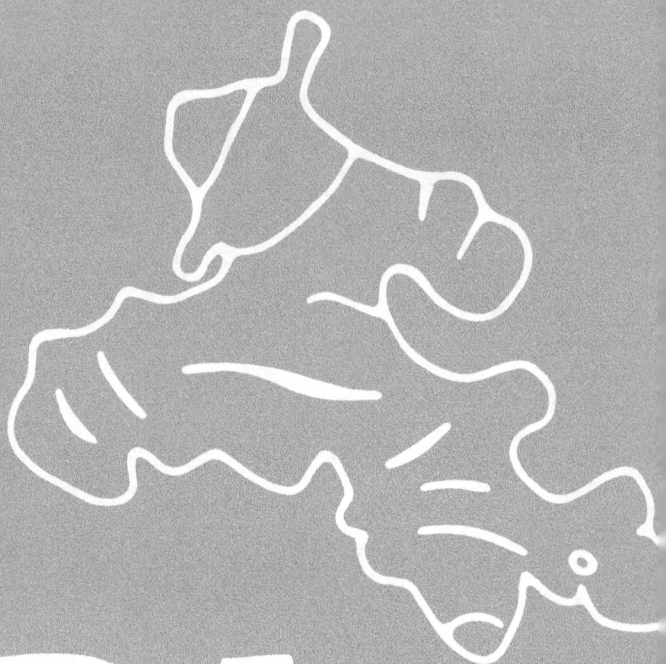

GINGER RUM

Fresh ginger is a fabulously spicy addition to spirits, and works especially well with rum. A dark, spiced rum will really complement the distinctive taste of fresh ginger, or you could use a lighter white rum for a more subtle liqueur. Ginger rum is delicious on its own, but also makes a wonderful cocktail ingredient when mixed with ginger beer and a generous squeeze of lime juice.

Ginger Rum

Ingredients
2 tbsp fresh ginger
3 cups rum

Method
1. Carefully chop your fresh ginger into chunks. Do not make the chunks too small, and do not remove the skin as it retains a lot of the flavour.

2. Put the chopped ginger into a sterilised bottle.

3. Top up the bottle with the rum, and seal it immediately.

4. Leave the ginger rum to infuse for a minimum of 3 days; the longer it is left, the stronger the flavour will be.

HERBS

Herbs are a wonderful addition to your homemade liqueurs, and can add a subtle and aromatic flavour to your final product. Caraway is a herb that has been found in ancient foods, and is still widely used today. The name comes from the Arabic word for the seed, karawya. Caraway has a sweet taste, making it the perfect ingredient to add to your homemade liqueur.

Caraway Vodka

Ingredients

4 cups vodka
1 tbsp caraway seeds

Method

1. Simply place the seeds into a sterilised bottle and top up with vodka.

2. Leave the liqueur to infuse for a minimum of two weeks, turning the bottles every other day to assist infusion.

3. Carefully strain your liqueur using a clean muslin cloth, or coffee filter paper.

4. Store in a sterilised bottle.

INFUSE

When making liqueurs at home, the key part of the process is infusion. Also called steeping, infusing is when you allow the base spirit you are using to take on the colours and flavours of what you are infusing it with. This process can take anywhere up to six months, and each recipe will have varying infusing times.

You may also want to monitor the infusion process by tasting your liqueur at regular intervals as it infuses. The time it takes for liqueurs to infuse varies widely from recipe to recipe, and taste testing ensures your liqueur is made to your taste. Most liqueurs will require filtering before serving, to strain out the ingredients you have infused your spirit with.

JELLY BEANS

Infusing your spirit with sweets is a fun and innovative way to add flavour and colour to your liqueur. Jelly beans are a great sweet to use, as their vibrant colours and variety of flavours can allow you to make a vast array of liqueurs. Try experimenting with mixtures of flavours, and see which combinations work best.

<u>Jelly Bean Vodka</u>

<u>Ingredients</u>
1 cup jelly beans
4 cups vodka

<u>Method</u>

1. Simply place the jelly beans into a sterilised bottle and top up with vodka.

2. Leave the liqueur to infuse for a minimum of two weeks, turning the bottles every other day to assist infusion.

K

KOLA KUBES

Kola Kubes are another sweet-shop favourite which work wonderfully as a flavour in homemade liqueurs. Kola kubes will give your liqueur a distinctive cola-like flavour, making it a perfect drink to enjoy on its own, or alongside a cola mixer.

Kola Kube Vodka

Ingredients
1 cup kola kubes
4 cups vodka

Method
1. Simply place the kola kubes into a sterilised bottle and top up with vodka.

2. Leave the liqueur to infuse for a minimum of two weeks, turning the bottles every other day to assist infusion.

LIMONCELLO

Limoncello is a fresh, zesty liqueur made with lemons. Limoncello is an Italian liqueur, widely enjoyed in Southern Italy. Traditionally, Limoncello is made from the zest of Femminello St. Teresa lemons, also known as Sorrento lemons or Sfusato Lemons, but you can use any lemons you like in this straightforward recipe for lemon liqueur.

Lemon Liqueur

Ingredients
Zest of 6 or 7 large organic lemons
1 litre vodka
5 cups water
3 cups sugar

Method
1. Carefully peel the zest from the lemons, avoiding the bitter white pith of the lemon skin.

2. Place the zest into a sterilised bottle, topping up with the vodka, and seal immediately.

3. Store the bottled liquid in a cool place and leave to steep for a week.

4. After the 7 days, boil the water and add the sugar to the boiling water. Stir the sugar until it is fully dissolved in the water, and allow the liquid to cool.

5. Strain the lemon peel from the alcohol and discard the peels.

6. Pour the sugar syrup into the glass jar with the alcohol and stir well.

7. Store your liqueur in the fridge.

M

MINT

Mint-infused liqueurs are a quirky and original digestif to offer guests after a meal as an alternative to a classic after-dinner mint. Adding minty sweets to a vodka base makes for an unusual and delicious liqueur. Try this simple recipe for mint vodka which uses mint imperials, the perfect sweet to use to make a refreshing liqueur.

Mint Imperial Vodka

Ingredients
1 cup mint imperials
4 cups vodka

Method
1. Simply place the mints into a sterilised bottle and top up with vodka. Seal the bottle immediately.

2. Leave the liqueur to infuse for a minimum of two weeks, turning the bottles every other day to assist infusion.

N

NUTS

Nuts are a fabulous addition to a spirit base, and once steeped, your nut-infused liqueur will make a fantastic ingredient to many a cocktail. We do not recommend eating the nuts after they have been used to infuse your vodka, as they will have absorbed a lot of alcohol.

Peanut Vodka.

Ingredients
1 cups unsalted peanuts
3 cups vodka

Method
1. Place your unsalted peanuts into a sterilised bottle.

2. Now, fill the bottle with vodka and quickly seal the top.

3. Leave the vodka to infuse for a minimum of two weeks; the longer the liqueur is left the stronger the flavour will be.

4. Strain the peanuts out of the vodka before serving it.

OUZO

Ouzo is a traditional Greek and Cypriot anise-flavoured liqueur, which is often enjoyed as an aperitif. It is very easy to make an anise-infused liqueur at home, and it can be consumed neat, or diluted with water as a longer drink, much like the traditional French anise-flavoured aperitif, Pastis. We recommend using vodka for this recipe, although any clear spirit, such as gin or white rum will work well, too.

Anise Liqueur

Ingredients
1/4 cup of green anise seed
1/8 cup coriander seed
1/2 tsp cinnamon
1/2 tsp mace
4 cups vodka

Method

1. Place all the ingredients in a sterilised bottle, or bottles.

2. Seal your bottles immediately.

3. Leave your liqueur to infuse in a cool place.

4. Allow your liqueur to infuse for a minimum of a month. The longer you leave it, the stronger the flavour will be.

5. Filter your liqueur before serving, using a clean muslin cloth, or coffee filter paper.

P

PEAR DROPS

Pear drops are another sweet-shop favourite which work wonderfully as a flavour in homemade liqueurs. Their distinctive flavour, and vibrant colour creates a lovely jewel-toned liqueur which can be enjoyed on its own, or as a long drink when mixed with soda water.

Pear Drops

Ingredients
1 cup pear drops
4 cups vodka

Method
1. Simply place the pear drops into a sterilised bottle and top up with vodka. Seal the bottle immediately.

2. Leave the liqueur to infuse for a minimum of two weeks, turning the bottles every other day to assist infusion.

QUINCE

Quince are small fruits which belong to the same family as pears. Quince trees are often grown for their pretty pink flowers, but the fruits can be used in jams and preserves, too.

The distinctive flavour of quince is a wonderful addition to whisky, creating a rich, malty liqueur. Try this traditional recipe for quince whisky, which makes a perfect warming tipple for a cold evening.

Quince Whisky

Ingredients

1 lb quinces
3 tbsp caster sugar
1 cinnamon stick
1 pint whisky

Method

1. Peel and grate the quinces into a large bowl, and sprinkle over 2 tablespoons of the sugar.

2. Leave the quinces and sugar to steep for 24 hours, then strain the juice through a clean muslin cloth, or coffee filter.

3. Add the cinnamon and the rest of the sugar to your quince juice, and pour the mixture into a sterilised bottle.

4. Add the whisky to the bottle, and seal immediately.

5. Leave your liqueur to infuse for three weeks, and filter again using a clean muslin cloth or coffee filter paper before serving.

RASPBERRY

The sweetness of raspberries work perfectly alongside a whisky base, complementing the malty flavour wonderfully. This recipe for raspberry whisky is an old favourite, and the addition of sugar alongside the fruit makes for a surprisingly sweet liqueur that even non-whisky drinkers will be sure to love.

Raspberry Whisky

Ingredients
2 cups raspberries
1 cup sugar
6 cups whisky

Method
1. In a bowl, mash the raspberries and sprinkle the sugar over the top.

2. Cover the bowl with a clean cloth and allow the mixture to stand for 24 hours.

3. Using a square of clean muslin, sieve the raspberry mixture to get rid of the seeds.

4. Carefully pour this mixture into a sterilised bottle, topping up the bottle with whisky.

5. Leave the liqueur to infuse for a minimum of three days.

SLOE GIN

Sloe gin is a popular drink, and a wonderful way to utilise these delicious little fruits. Sloes are from the same fruit-family as plums, and are found in abundance in the English countryside during the autumn months. A little sugar in this recipe helps release the rich sloe juices, and after a few months of infusing, you will be left with a wonderfully warming, syrupy drink. This recipe states to leave the liqueur to infuse for three months, but there is no upper time limit; the longer you can leave it, the better this liqueur will taste.

Sloe Gin

Ingredients
1 cup ripe sloes
1 tbsp sugar
3 cups gin

Method
1. Carefully prick your sloes with a needle, and place them in a sterilised bottle with the sugar.

2. Top the bottle up with gin, and seal immediately.

3. Leave your liqueur to infuse for a minimum of three months, shaking the bottle every week or so to assist infusion.

4. Serve; no need to strain.

TEA

Flavouring a base spirit with tea is a great way to infuse your liqueur with a subtle taste and distinctive aroma. The great thing about using tea to flavour your liqueur is that infusion is very quick, compared to some of the other recipes in this book. Adding to this, as the flavours are already encased in a tea bag, you will not need to filter or strain your liqueur before you drink it, you can simply remove the bags.

Earl Grey Gin

Ingredients
4 Earl Grey tea bags
4 cups gin

Method
1. Simply place your tea bags in sterilised bottles, and top up with the gin.

2. Seal the bottles immediately, and set aside somewhere cool.

3. Leave your liqueur to infuse for 6-8 hours. Do not leave for longer than 8 hours, or the liqueur may take on a bitter taste.

4. Remove the tea bags. Your liqueur is now ready to serve.

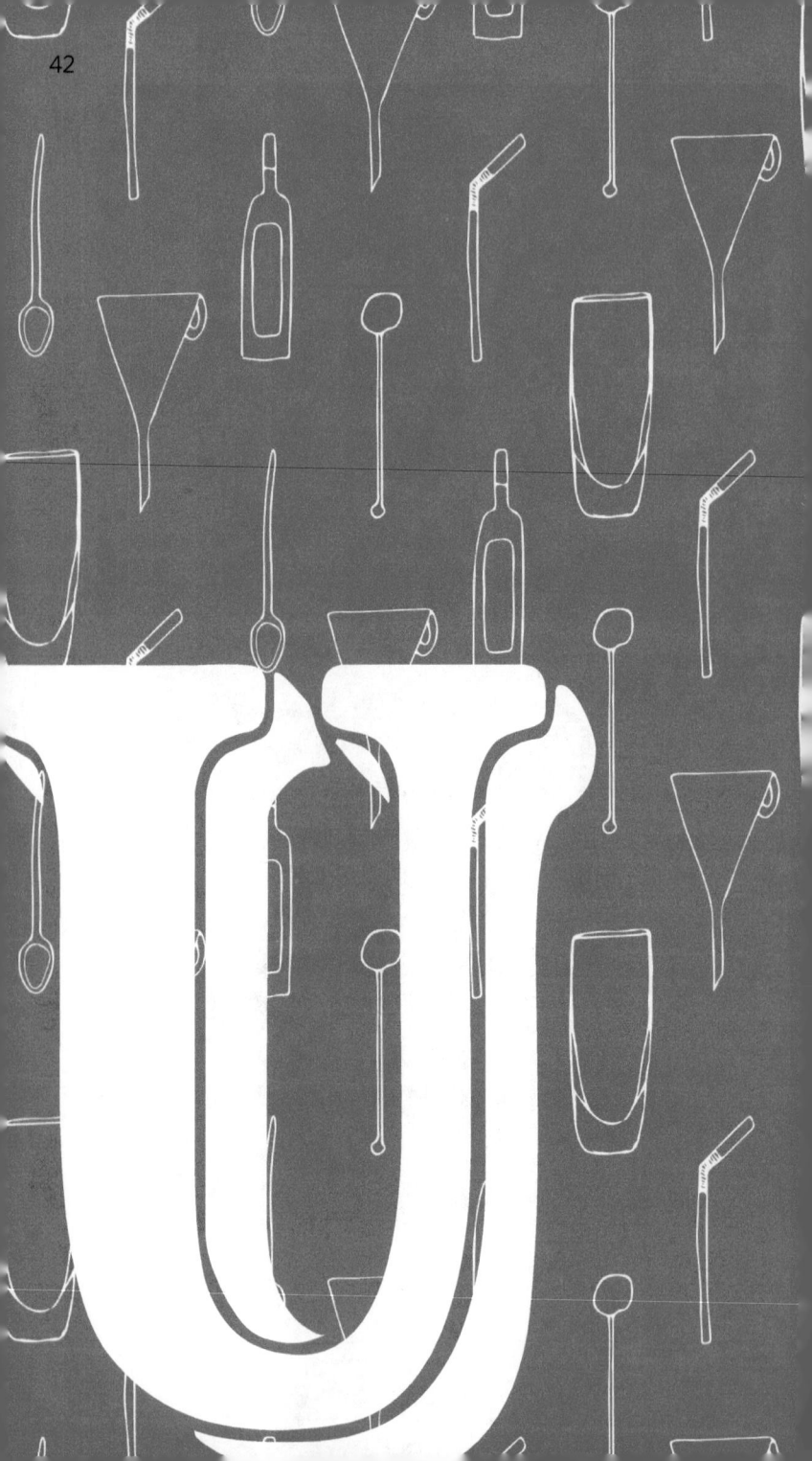

U

UTENSILS

The utensils you will need to make liqueur at home are rather basic, and easy to come by. You will need a selection of glass bottles. Glass demijohns or recycled glass bottles are great for making liqueur, and you can decant your finished product into smaller bottles to serve it, if you wish. A saucepan and wooden spoon will be necessary for a number of recipes which involve heating your ingredients before bottling, but most will not require any heating pre-infusion.

Straining or filtering your liqueur is an important part of the process; many recipes use a number of ingredients which should be removed before serving, both to preserve the delicious flavours, and to make the liqueur more aesthetically pleasing. You'll need to source some muslin cloths, or coffee filter papers to strain your liqueur, and a funnel will help you strain the liqueur without risking any spills!

VIOLET VODKA

Edible flowers are a lovely addition to your homemade liqueur, infusing your base spirit with a subtle, aromatic flavour. Wild flowers, such as violets, can be found in abundance at the right time of year, and you can gather handfuls of them for no cost. However, you must check that the flowers you pick are edible, and only pick them if there are an abundance; be considerate and remember to leave flowers for everyone to enjoy.

Violet Vodka

Ingredients
1 cup violets, stems removed
2 cups sugar
4 cups vodka
7 cups cooled, boiled water

Method
1. Place the violets into a sterilised bottle with the alcohol and seal immediately. Leave the flowers to infuse for 12 hours.

2. Gently heat the sugar and the water in a small saucepan over a low heat until the sugar has dissolved, and allow the mixture to cool.

3. Remove the violets from the vodka, and using the back of a spoon, crush them into a pulp.

4. Add the violet pulp to the sugar solution and carefully pour this mixture into a bottle to steep for 12 hours.

5. Mix the alcohol and sugar solution together, and filter your liqueur with a clean muslin cloth or coffee filter paper.

6. Bottle and store your liqueur for at least a month before serving.

WASABI VODKA

Here's a recipe for spice lovers! The distinctive, fiery flavour of wasabi is a daring and delicious addition to vodka, and will leave you with a powerfully-flavoured liqueur. Wasabi is part of the Brassicaceae family, which also includes horseradish and mustard. Indeed, wasabi is often referred to as Japanese horseradish. You could serve this unusual liqueur alongside Japanese food, for a quirky alternative to sake.

<u>Wasabi Vodka</u>

<u>Ingredients</u>
4 cups vodka
4 tsp wasabi paste

<u>Method</u>
1. Simply place your ingredients into a sterilised bottle, and seal immediately.

2. Shake the bottle to blend the ingredients, and leave the liqueur to infuse for a minimum of 7 days.

3. Shake the bottle of liqueur daily, to assist infusion.

XMAS

Christmas is the perfect time to enjoy your homemade liqueurs. Offering guests a festive drink you have made yourself is a lovely, personal touch which will make your Christmas parties all the more memorable. A whisky-based liqueur, complemented with a Christmas spice such as cinnamon is a perfect festive beverage, and once decanted into little bottles makes a thoughtful and original gift. Try this simple recipe for spiced Christmas liqueur.

Christmas Liqueur

Ingredients
6 oz sugar
4 oz cinnamon sticks, bruised
4 cups whisky

Method
1. Simply place your ingredients into a sterilised bottle, and seal immediately.

2. Shake the bottle to blend the ingredients, and leave the liqueur to infuse for a minimum of 10 days.

3. Shake the bottle of liqueur daily, to assist infusion.

4. Carefully filter your liqueur with a clean muslin cloth or coffee filter paper.

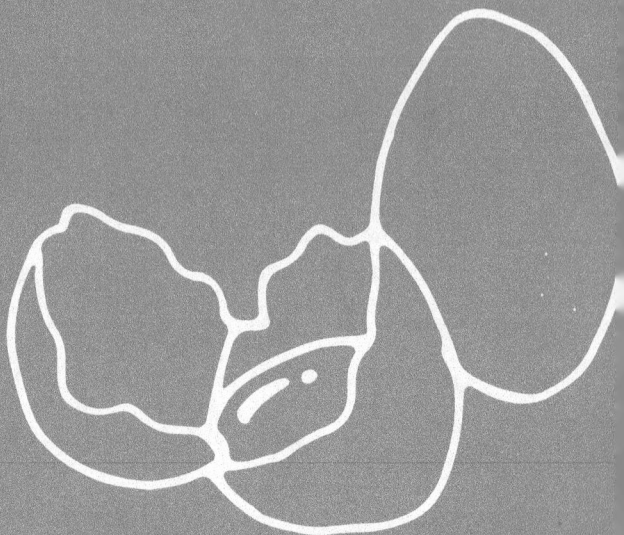

YOLK

Making liqueur with egg yolks, and eggs creates a wonderfully thick and creamy drink. Advocaat is the most renowned egg-based liqueur, and is a traditional Dutch alcoholic beverage. Egg yolks will give your liqueur a rich and creamy consistency, and distinctive custard-like flavour. Try this simple recipe for delicious egg-based brandy liqueur.

Egg Liqueur

Ingredients
2 egg yolks
2 eggs
4 cups icing sugar
3 cups brandy
5 cups whipping cream

Method
1. In a large bowl, whisk the eggs and egg yolks until they are frothy.

2. Sift the powdered sugar into the bowl gradually.

3. Add the alcohol and stir well.

4. Beat the whipping cream until slightly stiff and add this to the egg liqueur.

5. Pour the mixture into a sterilised bottle, and store in the fridge until serving.

ZEST

Adding the zest of citrus fruits to your liqueur is a wonderful way to add zingy flavour to a whole range of base spirits. Vodka works well as a base for your zesty liqueur, as the clear liquid contrasts with the vibrant fruit peel. A tangle of orange zest at the bottom of your bottle of liqueur looks rather lovely, and you can experiment with using lime, lemon, grapefruit and orange, or a mixture of these fruit peels.

Orange Vodka

Ingredients
The zest of one orange
1/2 cup sugar
4 cups vodka

Method
1. Carefully chop your orange zest into small strands, ensuring that you trim away any pith from the peel.

2. Place the zest and sugar into a sterilised bottle, and top up with vodka. Seal the bottle immediately.

3. Leave the liqueur to infuse for a minimum of two weeks, turning the bottles every other day to assist infusion.

TOP TEN TIP

1. Baby sterilising powder is a failsafe method of ensuring your bottles are safe to use

2. Making batches of liqueur throughout the year means you will always have a supply of homemade liqueur available.

3. Prepare in advance. If you need your liqueur ready for a particular occasion check the recipe well in advance and make sure you leave plenty of time for infusion.

4. Using seasonal fruits in your liqueur is a great way of utilising and preserving fruits when in abundance.

5. When using boiled sweets to infuse your base spirit, you can speed up the process dramatically by using a dishwasher. Put your sealed bottles in the dishwasher on a low heat, and the heat from the water will melt the sweets slightly, releasing their flavour and colour into the base spirit. Allow to cool thoroughly before consuming and be sure to use a low heat or the glass may shatter.

ND TRICKS

6. If you don't have a dishwasher, you can use a bowl of very hot water to help speed up infusion. Submerge the bottles in hot water until the water has cooled. Allow to cool thoroughly before consuming.

7. For best results in liqueur making, store your bottles in a cool, dark place out of direct sunlight. This will also allow them to keep for much longer.

8. Be on the lookout for decorative decanters and dainty little liqueur glasses to serve your liqueur in; secondhand shops and antique fairs are a good place to look.

9. Personalise your glass bottles with a handwritten label to make a bottle of homemade liqueur into a wonderful gift.

10. Always enjoy your homemade liqueur in moderation.

Two Magpies

Copyright © 2013 Two Magpies Publishing
An imprint of Read Publishing Ltd
Home Farm, 44 Evesham Road, Cookhill, Alcester,
Warwickshire, B49 5LJ

Commissioning Editor Rose Hewlett
Words by Sophie Berry
Design and Illustrations by Zoë Horn Haywood

British Library Cataloguing-in-Publication Data A
catalogue record for this book is available from the
British Library.

www.ingramcontent.com/pod-product-compliance
Lightning Source LLC
Chambersburg PA
CBHW051434090426
42737CB00014B/2967